ABOUT THE BOOK

When you attend a rodeo you have some small idea of the danger the contestants face. You surely feel the excitement of the event. But you probably don't have any idea at all about what the life of the Rodeo Rider is like.

Ms. Munn explores the life of the professional Rodeo contestant. She describes what it is like to go down the road on the suicide circuit. She examines every event, the stock, the travel, the winnings, the risk, the judging — in a word — the life.

Jerry Konst of Parker, Colorado at the National Little Britches Rodeo. Courtesy National Little Britches Rodeo Association.

RODEO RIDERS

Life on the Rodeo Circuit

By Vella c Munn

HARVEY HOUSE, Publishers
New York City, New York

Manufactured in the United States of America
ISBN 0-8178-0013-1
L.C. No. 80-81792

Harvey House, Publishers
20 Waterside Plaza
New York, New York, 10010

Published in Canada by
Fitzhenry & Whiteside, Ltd., Toronto

TABLE OF CONTENTS

Is there anyone who doesn't know what a cowboy is?

Not likely. The men who lived on horseback and looked after the wild cattle as they roamed the plains added a special chapter to our nation's history. What they did was unique.

Today it is easy to think of the cowboy as a romantic superhuman who thought like the horse he rode and was certain he was equal to the dangers around him. But it would be a strange man indeed who thought his life was romantic. Cold beans, jerky and biscuits without butter were his diet. Stampedes, storms, dry spells and times of near-starvation were his life. If he lost his horse he had lost everything. How could he get to water or shelter before Indians or wild animals found him?

Why did he do it? For one thing, in the early 1800s there were few ways for a man without money or land to earn a living. The West was waiting for someone strong enough to take it. Why not go where no one had gone before?

When he got there, he learned that law and order were back in the East. For years, cowboys lived or died by depending on how well they rode and used a gun — but it wasn't the gun that brought an end to the cowboy's way of life. It was the railroad. Trains helped write the final chapter on the need for men to look after wild, unpredictable cattle. Now barbed wire fences were doing the job it once took cowboys to handle, but cowboys didn't fade away. They changed with the times.

True, there are still a few who tend cattle for a living, but there are other kinds of cowboys too. Today men and women who ride or rope are known as rodeo contestants. What is a rodeo contestant? What does he or she do? Why?

The first two questions can be answered. The third isn't so easy. These are people who believe they can ride a sharp-hoofed bronc or lasso a frightened steer better or faster than anyone else at the rodeo. Some are teachers, truck drivers, or clerks. Only a handful are rodeo athletes.

Rodeo is a sport, but in one respect it is different from any other. In football, a man has to be stronger and quicker than his opponent standing in the way of making a touchdown, but at least that opponent is playing by the same rules.

Horses and bulls and steers don't know anything about rules. They don't want to be where they are. It's too noisy and people won't leave them alone. A few have been around so long they can second-guess the person on their back. Those are the dangerous ones, especially when it comes to the bulls. When all is said and done, rodeoing is a contest of human against animal.

Today's contestants come from everywhere. Some were brought up on the rodeo life because that's what others in their families did, while some come from cities that never hold rodeos. They are rich, poor and in-between. There are times, just as a cowboy settles down on the broad slippery back of a Brahma bull, when he asks why in tarnation he's there. Darn, he's scared. He can't forget the time when a bull stepped on his leg before the rodeo clown could get between them. But even if today's bull bucks him off, he gets up and heads for the next rodeo. Mountain climbers and treasure hunters keep on climbing or diving just because the mountain or sunken ship is there. The same holds true for professional rodeo riders.

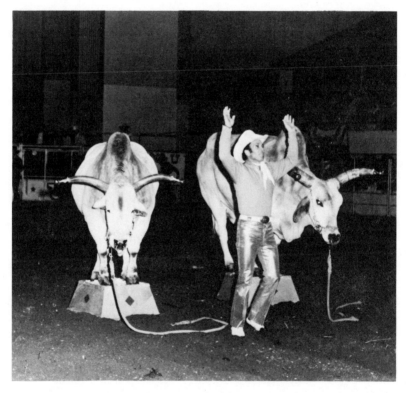

Not all Brahma bulls are used in the riding events. Sometimes they can be trained to perform.

Odds are, they'll never get rich. Even if a contestant doesn't end up hurt or crippled, there are only so many world champions like Tom Ferguson or Metha Bronson. But what else could they do? Drive a truck? That sounds kind of boring. Sell dresses? Who wants to be inside all the time? Besides, how many people can say they've ridden a 2,400-pound bull to the bell?

What is the rodeo life like anyway?

It's breathing in dust on a hot day and landing in the mud all spring. It's calloused hands that shake and have to be kept busy because you don't want your friends to know you're as nervous as they are. It's waking up stiff after a fall and riding with knee braces and knowing when you hit the ground that you've dislocated your shoulder — again. It's calling your family long-distance instead of being with them and crying because your prize barrel-racing horse broke its leg.

It isn't all bad. There is the good feeling that comes from knowing who Montie Montana is and choking up when a woman on a quarterhorse races in during the Grand Entry with the American flag streaming out behind her. It's seeing a silver buckle saying World Champion All Around Cowboy on a man named Larry Mahan and thinking he's the biggest man you've ever seen even if he weighs only 160 pounds. Mostly, though, it's wanting that buckle for yourself.

There are hundreds of rodeos in the United States and Canada a contestant can go to, and yet the only thing these rodeos really have in common is the anticipation that fills the air when the announcer booms out a welcome.

Each rodeo has its own special flavor. This stagecoach race at Pendleton, Oregon is part of what fans remember about the Old West.

For the contestant, every rodeo points toward one thing — making it to the finals. Oklahoma City is where the year's Professional Rodeo Cowboys Association championships for men are decided and $200,000 worth of prize money given out each December. No matter what happened during the year, if a man can get there, he's one of the greats. He knows it was worth it. And so do the 89,000 fans who've paid to watch the show. The ten top cowboys in each event are matched with the top riding animals in ten performances of fast-paced rodeo that leaves most cowboys so exhausted they're not sure they can ever get up again.

At the PRCA finals, women are limited to barrel racing, but those who rope steers or calves or ride bucking stock compete as members of the Womens Professional Rodeo Association or International Rodeo Association. When the finals are over, win or lose, every contestant has ridden his or her heart out. The champions have been decided, prize money distributed, and pictures taken. The suicide circuit is over.

At least it is for a few weeks. Then down in Texas around the end of January the whole thing starts all over again. The hundreds of contestants who didn't make it to the finals last year are gearing up for the long haul. They put on their Stetsons, throw a gear bag over their shoulders, and head on down the road. It may just be the roughest job in the world, but it's theirs.

This is the suicide circuit.

Who was the first cowboy? That's the same as asking the name of the first wild horse. The only thing we know for sure is that wild horses and long-horned cattle were here and waiting when cowboys first rode across the Southwest. In the early 1800s, the horses and cattle left behind by Spanish *conquistadores* were multiplying at a great rate. They had few natural enemies and the hundreds of miles of prairie could support large herds. A cowboy could live off cattle and horses.

At first there were only a few dusty, sunburned men doing their darndest to tame a horse so they could ride herd on the skiddish, stubborn longhorn cattle. Except for horses and cattle and assorted coyotes, cougars, buffalo and Indians, cowboys were the only living things for hundreds of miles around.

They used more than the animals the Spanish had left behind. They also became experts at handling *la reata* — the lariat. With a rope, a man could capture a horse and tie down a bellowing calf long enough to put a brand on it. A cowboy learned how to use his rope, fast. It was either that or be left alone and afoot a thousand miles from the nearest settlement.

It was a hard, lonely life. A man who didn't have quick wits, courage, roping and riding skills didn't live long. There were no books, newspapers or mail from home to take a man's thoughts from what he was doing. No wonder he looked forward to the cattle drives. It was the only chance to see people and catch up on what was going on in the world. When cowboys got together, a lot of boasting went on about who could ride a newly captured horse, and these boasts turned into contests that were the start of today's rodeos.

As far as anyone knows, the first real rodeo was held in Pecos, Texas in 1883. Cowboys showed up to pit themselves against each other for prize money donated by a group of businessmen. At first, people watched for free but on the Fourth of July, 1887, in Prescott, Arizona, spectators were charged a fee. It wasn't long before other towns saw that Prescott had a good idea.

William F. Cody took a look at the rodeos and added his own touch. He organized Buffalo Bill's Wild West show. The Miller Brothers' Wild West show went one step further by featuring Lucille Mulhol, the first cowgirl. She had been raised on a ranch, and used her skills to become a champion in roping and tying steers.

The early rodeos were pretty wild. It wasn't unheard of for a promoter, the man or men responsible for putting a rodeo together, to skip out of town without paying the winners. In addition, there were no standards for judging the different bucking and roping events. One cowboy might find himself asked to lasso a 400-pound calf, while another easily roped and tied one weighing closer to 200 pounds. How could anyone decide the winner in a contest like that?

The managers of several of the leading rodeos formed the International Rodeo Management to work on the problems. It was a start in the right direction, but the organization could only make suggestions. At the same time, the cowboys were changing. They wanted to be able to make a living without worrying about whether they were going to be judged fairly. It was time to civilize rodeos. That happened in 1936 at the Boston Garden when cowboys went on strike and demanded they be given some rights. Finally the producers gave in to the demands and the rodeo was held.

This is where a clown really earns his money. The cowboy hightails it for safety while the bull zeroes in on the clown. On the ground is the rope the cowboy held onto during his ride.

Soon the few women who were competing decided they were tired of being treated as oddities. They wanted to compete against each other in their own events. Barrel racing, the women's only event, was accepted as a legitimate rodeo contest. Not content with that, women took one look at the Professional Rodeo Cowboys Association (for men only) and formed the Girls Rodeo Association (now the Womens Professional Rodeo Association).

Rodeo today is still changing, with hopes of becoming better. Thanks to animal humane groups, the bucking and roping stock are treated like prized animals. They even have their own bucking champions.

Today strong, competent athletes can make a living as rodeo contestants. They have their own newspapers, a telephone-recorded hotline which gives up-to-the-minute rodeo news, even television coverage of the largest rodeos.

Nothing comes close to the rodeo way of life. We live in a mechanized world. We are ruled by stop lights, the nearest policeman, how much money we have. But when an athlete settles down on a Brahma bull, laws have nothing to do with what's going to happen.

If there's one thing rodeo contestants have in common, it's that they spend a lot of time traveling. What is it like to run to two, three, or more rodeos a week? For one thing, it wears a person out. That's why contestants look for a traveling partner or accept an invitation to pile into a car filled with others headed for the same rodeo. Another reason for having someone else along is to save money. Inflation has hit the professional contestant. True, those 620 PRCA rodeos paid out over $8.5 million last year, but it costs more to live on the road now.

Then there's the expense of feed for a roping or barrel-racing horse, motel rooms, airplane tickets, and equipment. A bucking saddle can cost over $350, chaps start at $50, and bareback rigging goes for at least $90, to say nothing of the cost of entry fees for the rodeos.

How does a newcomer get on the professional rodeo circuit? In some sports the ladder up starts in college when the best players are watched by professional scouts as possible draft choices. People like Tracy Austin and Kareem Abdub-Jabbar are written about before they're ready to turn professional and, when the time comes, they sign contracts for thousands, sometimes millions, of dollars. Rodeo contestants are on their own. Rodeoing can start at as young an age as eight. Both the American Junior Rodeo Association and Little Britches Rodeo are for youngsters through their teen years. In Little Britches the rules are almost identical to those of the PRCA and WPRA. Girls don't participate in the bucking events but ride and rope. In AJRA they are allowed to do everything boys do. High school rodeoing is growing and a teenager may decide to go to one of the nearly 100 colleges that belong to the National Intercollegiate Rodeo Association where they can concentrate on riding and roping skills and test themselves at the national college finals.

There's nothing that says a boy or girl has to go to college to learn to rodeo. Some rodeo pros hold bucking schools. Anyone who has the money can take lessons from Don and Pete Gay, Monty Henson or Larry Mahan. It costs from $135 to $200 to attend the schools but for many it's worth every penny.

Becoming what's called a permittee is usually the first step. That's no more complicated than sending in an application and the necessary fees. In return, the new member is allowed to ride in all approved rodeos. After certain requirements have been met, they are eligible for regular membership as professionals.

Although being a professional means living on the road, it's not quite as frantic as it first sounds. The circuit is centered around certain parts of the country at different times of the year. Texas is the place to be for the January and February rodeos — then much of the nation is so cold a contestant couldn't hold onto a rope. As the weather

18

warms, the circuit spreads north and westward, but things don't bust loose until summer. That's when most rodeos are planned. It isn't unusual for a contestant to be entered in four or five rodeos over a period of three days. Even youngsters often attend as many as three rodeos a week.

It is essential for a contestant to be organized. For every animal ridden or roped, a contestant has to pay an entry fee. If the check doesn't get there on time or a contestant is stuck in traffic when it's time to ride, there goes the money. The organizations frown on contestants who can't be depended on. For example, a PRCA member who doesn't pay his entry fee by the end of the first go-round is fined $100 the first time and $200 if it happens again. After that he's suspended.

Rodeoing is a sport for the young and strong. Ann Lewis was the world champion barrel racer at the age of ten. Jackie Jo Perrin didn't win that title until she was 13, but she did start barrel racing when she was seven. The emphasis on youth is true of most sports. Why else would Allen Watkins be barrel racing, pole bending and steer riding at six? No other athlete faces the risk of serious injury as much as those who rodeo. In fact, the chance of injury is so great there isn't an insurance company that will let a cowboy or cowgirl sign on the dotted line. Contestants have their own health insurance. It pays the bill for stitches and casts, but if a contestant becomes disabled there is trouble.

Because rodeoing is hardly something people can do until they're 65, the contestants have to start looking around for other ways of making a living while they're still on the circuit. If they're at the top they may use their names in advertising. There are Joe Alexander Spurs, Larry Mahan's cowboy clothing, and Monty Henson's saddles.

There are only a few pulling in really big money. Jackie Jo Perrin won $12,000 during the season and an additional $3,610 at the finals, hardly a world-shattering amount. Just the same, there isn't much chance people will stop being lured by the call of the rodeo. Rodeo is a magic world which appeals because it reminds us of the days when there weren't any fences or stop lights or alarm clocks.

At a rodeo people can forget there's anything except wild horses, Brahma bulls and young men and women in Western hats hanging over wooden fences. Youngsters lean forward in their seats and know there's nothing they'd rather do than be waiting their turn to come out of the next gate.

What does a clown do? Seth Doulton's job here is to distract the bull while the cowboys scramble for the fence.

BULL RIDING — THE BIG EVENT

It was December, 1976. Twenty-three-year-old Don Gay was going after his third straight bull-riding championship. He drew Red One, a tough bull on its way to being judged best bucker at the finals. With Don was his brother Pete, another bull rider, and father Neil, a former bronc rider turned promoter. But when Don came out of the chute he was alone.

Eight seconds later Don had ridden for 95 points, the highest ever given a bull rider at the finals.

Why do people go to a rodeo? One answer tops them all — to see the bulls. When a bull explodes from the chute with a stiff-armed contestant clinging to its broad back with heels and knees and thighs, every eye is on the action. Where else is a fan going to see a 160-pound man or 120-pound woman try to ride up to 2,400 pounds of muscle and horn?

General Isomo, who was bull of the year, can fool a rider. He has a reputation as an easy keeper with a pleasant personality. He has one bad habit, though. He doesn't like to stay home and there's hardly a fence he can't jump. One other thing — only six cowboys out of 25 rode him to the bell that year.

More contestants are injured in the bull-riding event than any other. If nothing else, the riding arm is going to feel like it tried to stop a train single-handed. Wacy Cathey's bull robbed him of his front teeth and Randy Meyers suffered cracked ribs and a mild concussion at the same finals.

Yet there are more men ready to climb into a chute with a snorting, thick-horned bull than a bronc. Why? Well, for one thing, there's no disgrace in being thrown off an animal whose skin can move 30 degrees in either direction. In fact, more bull riders get bucked off than make it to the bell. Strength is about the only thing that keeps a man going in the same direction as the animal under him.

Cowgirls handle bull riding a little differently. Their rules call for them to stay on for six seconds instead of eight and they can decide beforehand whether they want to use one or two hands. They don't have to spur, but the score will go up if they do. Doesn't that make it easier for women? Don't say that to Karen Christianson. She was thrown from a 1,500-pound bull during the last night of the GRA finals, had her jaw broken and was knocked unconscious when the bull hit her face.

From first appearances, bull riding looks like an individual effort. Oh, there's the flanker who buckles on the broad flank strap designed to irritate the bull and the friend who pulls the bull rope tight at the last moment. But as soon as the contestant is out of the chute, it's human against bull. Unlike the bronc events, there are no riders waiting to help a contestant off a bull. It's too dangerous. A bull is as likely to charge a horse as a human. And a quarterhorse is too valuable to risk having close to those horns. When a contestant decides to bail off or the bull does the job, the arena is a lonely place to be.

Then help comes. Many fans think the clown is there for comedy relief. But a rodeo clown has the most serious job in the rodeo world. He wouldn't be wearing spiked baseball shoes if he didn't have to be sure on his feet. He's all that stands between a downed rider and those hooves and horns and nasty temper.

What makes a bull buck? Sure they're born with a mean streak, but to make things more exciting, the bull owners want the "rankest" they can find. The bull that bucks, hooks, twists, and spins, all at the same time if possible, is the one they want. But a contestant can't depend on a bull's disposition to be assured of a money-making ride. That's why the rules call for a clanging cowbell hanging between the bull's legs. What animal is going to put up with that nonsense? The bell is held in place by a long flat rope that goes around the bull's stomach and has a handhold braided in it for the contestant to grip. During the ride the hand holds the rope tight against the animal but at the end of the ride or when the contestant is bucked off, the bell's weight pulls the rope away from the contestant's loosened hand.

At least that's the way it's supposed to work. In order to get a firm hold, a contestant grips the rope as tightly as possible by wrapping it around the gloved palm several times. If the contestant should happen to be flipped forward, fingers can get twisted in the rope, and that's one mighty dangerous position to be in.

More than the bell irritates the bull. The flank strap, a broad band of leather around the bull's belly is tightened at the last minute. The contestant is wearing spurs and the shaft of each dull spur is bent inward to help the rider get a grip on that slipping, sliding skin.

There are rules to bull riding but, since bulls can't read the rule book, the burden falls on the contestants — they've got to remain civilized on an uncivilized animal. But unless they're hurt too badly to pull their boots on, they'll probably keep on getting on those ornery animals.

And why not? What else can come close to bull riding for excitement?

No wonder bucking saddles don't have the high horns regular saddles do. That could result in a painful landing.

Learning the rules of bull riding are a snap compared to what goes through a contestant's mind while getting ready to put a saddle on a horse. Luckily the contestant has help. All around are others who will do everything they can to come up with a better ride, but they don't mind lending a hand. Pretty soon it is going to be the other contestant's turn, and a little help makes the job easier.

"Where do I take him?" is an important question. That means the contestant wants some opinion on where to wrap a hand around the bucking rope attached to a halter. Some horses buck with their heads tucked between their legs, while others act like they're trying to reach the sun. If a contestant hasn't ridden this horse before, he or she finds someone who has. Then the contestant is told whether to take a close grip on the rope or give the horse a little leeway. Of course there's always the chance the horse will do what no one expected it to do.

Before a ride the contestant shakes the horn of the specially built association saddle that cost at least $300 to make sure it's on tight and sticks booted feet in the stirrups. Years ago cowboys pulled their working saddles off their own horses and went right to rodeoing on them, but today's saddle is fairly flat with little or no horn. Although it is harder to stay on, a contestant is less likely to be bruised on a high ridge or stabbed by a horn.

Just before the gate is opened, the saddle is cinched tight and the flank strap pulled up. The contestant takes a grip on the braided hemp rope and takes a deep breath, legs held high so that the spurs are over the horse's shoulders.

The moment a cowboy comes out of the chute he is raking his dull spurs along the horse's neck in sweeps timed with the horse's bucks. It's murder on the knees, but it's either ride by the rules or wind up with no score. His free hand is high in the air. If it touches the horse the judges will turn their backs even if he stays on for the required ten seconds.

Cowgirls go out for a six-second ride. Before the event a woman can choose between one or two hands, but if she elects to use one hand she can't change to two after the ride begins. Her spurs must be in the horse's shoulders when she comes out of the chute or she loses ten points.

Since judges award both rider and horse points according to their performances, the horse a contestant draws is important. Angel Sings, a registered quarterhorse, went from being untrainable to the college rodeo world championship and finally saddle bronc of the year. An honest bucker, especially one who leaps high, lands hard and kicks out with its back legs, will take a contestant into the money. Not that an athlete has a say in the matter, since riders and horses are paired in a kind of lottery before the rodeo begins.

There's just one problem left once the ride is over. How is a contestant going to get off and back to safety? This is where the pickup men come in. It usually works like this. One rider comes up on the bronc's left while the other covers the right, trapping the animal between them. One rider ties the bucking rope around his saddle horn while the other rider lets the contestant climb on behind. Once the irritating strap near the horse's flank has been loosened the animal usually stops bucking and follows the other horses out of the arena so quietly fans sometimes wonder if the whole thing was rigged.

It wasn't. One look at the difference between a bronc and the steady animals the pickup men ride clarifies that. A prized quarterhorse gets a lot of loving care. A saddle bronc is left alone with its accumulation of dirt. Considering the way champion broncs are treated and how the rules tend to favor the four-footed participants, it's no wonder the saddle bronc event has the fewest contestants entered in it.

BAREBACK — DESIGNED FOR THE RODEO

When cowboys first climbed into arenas no one gave a thought to getting on a wild horse without putting a saddle on it first. That was one plumb crazy idea. But early promoters saw the bareback event as a way of adding extra spark to a rodeo.

When bareback riding first came into its own, contestants were allowed to hold on with both hands, but that almost tipped the scale in the contestant's favor. Nowadays a bareback bronc comes out of the chute wearing only a ten-inch-wide leather belt, which has a suitcase-type handle for the contestant to cling to, wrapped tightly around its midsection. There are no reins, no stirrups. Like bull rider Butch Kirby said after his first and only bareback ride, "Riding bareback is like grabbing hold of a freight train." Women can choose between riding with one hand or two but that doesn't make their job a lot easier.

Although it doesn't show at first, there's a difference between contestants who concentrate on the bareback event and those who tote a saddle around with them. By and large, bareback riders are a younger bunch because staying on a bronc with only a handhold between human and disaster takes a lot of strength. Judy Robinson was only 23 and in her first year of competing when she became all-around GRA champion. She took second in bareback, third in bull riding and first in steer undecorating. At 18 Danny Waggoner was the Little Britches All Around Champion concentrating on the bareback event. Danny plays football, basketball and track. He entered his first rodeo at eight and at last count had 15 trophy saddles, 85 other trophies and 190 buckles.

Judy and Danny are tough, but they're no more durable than the horses they find themselves pitted against. One year Sipping Velvet came out of the chute 38 times, but was ridden only once. The bronc was bred for one thing — bucking.

Put a strong, determined rider together with a small but shifty horse for the six or eight seconds the smaller bareback horse is considered to be in top form, and the result is a whale of a lot of action. Most riders practically sit on the hand they've wrapped around the handle. This position causes them to spur higher on the horse's neck than a saddle bronc rider does. Remember, a contestant has to spur the whole time. Another thing, if the free hand touches the horse or any part of the rigging, the judges are going to give the rider a goose egg for a score.

A bareback contestant is much less likely to be thrown than a bull rider and the event can turn into a series of impressive rides with only an experienced judge being able to sort the best from the near-best.

Pickup riders have the same responsibility as in the saddle bronc event but the rules change when there's no rope near the horse's head. About the only thing the riders can do is keep the bronc from charging around and give the contestant something solid to aim at when it comes time to bail off. Because the bronc has more freedom of movement, the contestant isn't the only one who has to be on guard. More than one pickup rider or horse bears hoof scars from a bronc who flipped around and connected with the nearest object. At least the broncs aren't looking to hurt anyone. Unlike the bulls, a horse doesn't hold a grudge against the humans around it. All it wants is to be left alone.

Considering the odds against a contestant, it's a wonder there are so many of them waiting to be flipped head over heels or have arms pulled out of their sockets. Johnny Trout was told he'd never move again after landing on his neck but he's on his feet again, and he still wants to rodeo.

A contestant can pay as much as $100 for the right to get on the back of a smelly, teeth-gnashing horse who might upend in the chute before things get underway. On top of that, the contestants know there's about one chance in four of getting the entry-fee money back.

Yep, it can get downright discouraging. Yet there's always the next rodeo, the thought that this time everything's going to come out the way it's supposed to. That's the thought that got Johnny Trout out of the hospital.

In most events cowgirls have to share the spotlight with men but, thanks to a group of women in Texas years ago, they have one event they can call their own — barrel racing. In Little Britches and AJRA boys compete in barrel racing but it isn't for men. That's tough for Allen Watkins who started barrel racing at six after seeing his 12-year-old brother Todd take the AJRA barrel-racing championship.

Actually, it isn't the brightly dressed cowgirls who make the event a success. It's their four-footed partners. On a fast, dependable horse, a girl no older than ten can become a world champion, which is exactly what Ann Lewis did back in the 1960's.

The event calls for a contestant to run her horse around a clover-leaf pattern. The idea is to cut as much time as possible from the run by coming close to three 55-gallon steel drums without knocking them over. From a distance it looks as though the horse is going to fall over as it leans toward the barrel. This has happened, but usually during the long training back home and not in the arena. Since a good barrel-racing horse can cost over $6,000, it's no wonder a cowgirl looks after her animal's needs before tending to her own.

Although a barrel racing horse often looks on the edge of disaster as it leans into the barrel, there are few spills.

Back in 1903 a black cowboy named Bill Pickett started steer wrestling when he used his strength instead of a rope to manhandle a steer that refused to go into a corral. What's the difference between someone who rides an animal and one who jumps off a quarterhorse to wrestle a 700-pound steer to the ground? Take a look at Bryon Walker and you have your answer. At 205 pounds, he has as good a chance of bringing one of those ornery critters to the ground as anyone. Of course if Billy Dale Haley turns from ribbon roping and tie-down roping to steer wrestling, Bryon might have to step aside. At 15, Billy weighed 252 pounds and stood six-feet-two-inches and was the reigning AJRA champion in his events.

But steer wrestling takes more than just strength. Any bulldogger will tell you it takes timing and smoothness and coordinated action, to say nothing of a cooperative steer. In the first place, the contestant has to hold his horse back until the steer has crossed what's called a score line. If he doesn't, the judges add a ten-second penalty to his time. Can't he make up the penalty with a quick throw? Well, not likely. A top dogger can bring a steer to the ground in four seconds.

Although only one contestant is after the steer, the event calls for two riders. The one bent on wrestling a steer to the ground is called the dogger, but he's lost without his hazzer who rides out on the opposite side of the steer to keep it going on a straight path. As soon as the dogger gets close enough to touch the steer's flank, he leans out of the saddle and reaches for that bouncing horn. Then it's time to commit himself to the job of tackling that steer.

Ideally, the cowboy lands a little ahead of the steer

Concentration and strength are essential if a cowboy hopes to muscle a steer off its feet.

and digs his heels into the ground. The idea is to tip the steer's head so far to the side that the animal is looking at the sky and so will lose its footing and flop over onto its side. All four feet and the head must be pointing in the same direction, a problem since the steer can tuck its feet under or twist its head in the opposite direction in a "dog fall."

More than that can go wrong. If a man hits the steer too hard the animal may be knocked over instead of twisted down. This is called a "houlihan." Then there's the chance one of those long horns will get twisted or "pegged" into the ground. Finally there's the steer who seems to have a mass of rubber for a neck. No matter how the cowboy strains or twists, the steer stands solidly on its feet, head turned halfway around. It's enough to make an adult cry.

A cowboy had better be able to depend on his horse. An animal who keeps up with a steer and mixes cow sense with second-guessing is worth its weight in gold. It isn't unusual for the same animal to chase a half-dozen steers in an afternoon, each time with a different cowboy who has paid rent money on the horse for the duration of the ride.

Considering the expense of having to travel with a horse and the care and attention such a valuable animal requires, is it worth it for a contestant to specialize in steer wrestling instead of the riding events where the contractors provide the animals? Well, ask Tom Ferguson. This seven-time All Around Cowboy won $120,000 one year by specializing in the steer-wrestling and calf-roping events.

*Steer wrestler Dave Brock demonstrates the split second timing
needed to connect with a steer instead of the ground.*

38

STEER UNDECORATING

Steer wrestling usually isn't an event for women since there aren't many of them who have the necessary strength. That doesn't mean steers are safe from cowgirls. There's always steer undecorating. What this means is that someone has taped or glued a ribbon to the back of a 700-pound steer and it's up to the cowgirl to get the ribbon off in record time. The steer is let into the arena with the contestant and her hazzer hot on the steer's heels. They have to guide the steer between them while the contestant reaches down and grabs the ribbon so she can get the judge to stop the time clock. The contestant gets only two chances to remove the ribbon, which means her horse has to be quick and sure-footed. No wonder. A top contestant can do the job in under two seconds.

In team roping the steer is given a head start. The header's job is to get a rope around the horns of a thousand pounds of running steer and pull it to a stop. The header then turns the steer back to the left while the heeler moves in to rope the hind legs.

When things go right, the roped steer is trapped between both contestants with both horses facing each other and the ropes taut. Between the two of them they have three chances to complete a throw, but retrieving a rope eats up precious time. Because the steers are big they can lunge against the rope and more than one roper has lost a finger by letting it get trapped between the saddle horn and rope.

This describes the California style of team roping. The Arizona style is most often seen in the Southwest. The difference is that both header and heeler are permitted two loops. The idea is to wind up with the steer's hind legs tied with either a square or granny knot. The steer must be on the ground and whether the contestant trips, stretches or tails it down doesn't matter. What does is the matter of time it takes.

Considering that steers have been roped in five

seconds, this means fancy teamwork. This event requires less physical strain on a contestant than other events and a roper can almost make a lifetime career out of running down a steer with a lasso. J.D. Yates roped in the finals with his father when he was 15. At that rate he might be around forever.

Cottom Rosser already has his rope over the steer's horn. Now it's son Lee's turn to rope the hind legs.

Although it doesn't show, there's a rope leading from the saddle horn to the calf's neck. In calf roping, the calf has to be on its feet and then the cowboy upends it and ties three feet together.

Next to breaking wild horses, steer roping reminds more people of the Western life than anything else and yet most rodeos no longer have steer roping as a scheduled event. "It's too hard on the steer," was the cry that led to the event falling into disfavor.

Yet it's easy to understand why contestants go on racing into arenas after full-grown steers. When everything works, steer roping looks easy, but putting a rope around a steer's horns from the back of a galloping horse is a skill that takes time to perfect. The idea is to get the rope around the steer's horns, race forward, and then lay the slack rope across the steer's back and around its rump. That's when the horse veers away, jerking the steer's head back.

That's what it takes to throw a steer off balance and onto the ground for a "fair catch." While the horse is skidding to a stop, the cowboy is off and racing to the steer. His job is to tie the steer before it can get back on its feet. He'd never make it if his horse didn't keep a taut rope between itself and the steer, making it impossible for the animal to regain its feet.

Two hundred pounds is a basic weight for a calf. Unfortunately, one that comes bawling into the arena at 350 pounds is also a calf and that calls for a little "umph" when it comes to dropping the animal to the ground, but it can be done. Before Roy Cooper's first year at the finals at 20 he'd been roping long enough and well enough to have collected 43 trophy saddles.

Like the other roping events, the action starts behind an automatic barrier. The calf goes first while the horse waits for a signal from the rider. The instant the barrier drops, contestant and horse are off. First the contestant has to snake a loop around the calf's head. Then the horse comes close to the calf, giving the contestant a clear shot at the critter's neck. That's when athlete and horse part company.

Wrapping a six-foot length of pigging string around three legs takes a little time. First the contestant has to be sure the calf is on its feet, and then upends it in any way that works. Almost before the calf hits the ground, the contestant is tying three legs together. Only, it's not over yet. The calf has five seconds in which to struggle against the rope. If the tie holds, the time is official. One rule is for the contestant and even then it isn't a great one! If the first rope thrown at the calf's head doesn't hold, the contestant may try again, but by then precious seconds are lost.

Women have added a new twist to calf roping called breakaway calf roping. Jackie Jo Perrin, 13-year-old barrel-racing champion, and her older sister Cindy have been so successful that Jackie has a good shot at a rodeo scholarship. In breakaway, the time ends when a roped calf jerks the rope off the saddle horn. The rope must pass over the calf's head and the contestant is allowed to carry two ropes in case the first rope fails.

At the moment there's plenty of slack in the rope but suddenly the calf will be pulled up short.

Goat roping — a popular Little Britches and AJRA event for everyone except the goat.

At first glance this event looks like someone's idea of a joke, but it's a popular event in Little Britches and AJRA. Some contestants are so young that they could only handle the smallest calves and that wouldn't be humane for the calves. Goats make a fiesty substitute. The goat is tied to a stake with a 15-foot rope and the contestant's job is to ride up to the goat, dismount, and throw the goat before tying its legs as in calf roping. The big problem is that a goat is one crazy animal. As it tries to get away, it runs in circles around its tether or even falls over before a rope touches it.

Another event using a goat is called tail tying and anyone who has done that knows how hard it is to hit a moving target. The goat is tethered to a stake and the contestant's job is to tie a ribbon around the goat's tail while the judge stands by with a stopwatch.

The person fans care about is the one coming out of chute #4 on a bull or bronc. But what if there weren't any bulls or broncs?

That's easy enough isn't it? Just bring in a truckload of bulls with humps on their shoulders and some horses no one has a use for — nothing to it. Hardly! For one thing, most horses don't buck the moment someone gets on their backs. One who flips its hind legs toward the sky is a rare creature indeed.

There are some 50 stock contractors on the lookout for horses and bulls, calves and steers. For them, owning champion bucking bulls and horses is worth the time spent looking for the one with the spark that causes it to do everything but turn inside out when a human settles down on it.

There isn't much glamour in being a stock contractor. Mostly it's putting up with animals who have no sense of appreciation. In addition, the contractor has to contend with stock trucks that break down, feed that doesn't arrive, and finding people to look after the critters.

Most contractors are in more than just the animal end of the rodeo business. The people who put a rodeo together rely on the contractor for many things. Often they don't have a public address system, and unless the fans can hear what the announcer is saying they're going to ask for their money back. Not only do contractors come up with sound systems, they usually provide an announcer who knows rodeos and contestants and can explain what's going on.

They're also responsible for an arena director to keep the show running in the middle of calamity. Stock has to be in position for an event, contestants have to be where they're supposed to be — that's the arena director's job.

The rodeo committee is made up of people who aren't experts on rules and regulations. That's why they ask the contractor to supply judges and timers. Usually, judges and timers are contestants who know from firsthand experience what constitutes a good bucking animal. Athletes who have been injured will take the job because it keeps them in spending money while they heal.

Another area where the contractor comes in handy is lining up contract acts. A contract act can be anything from trick and fancy ropers and riders to clowns and trained animals. These talented people provide entertainment during breaks in the rodeo. Sometimes it's hard to know which is more dangerous, being a contestant or racing around in a brilliant costume with your head hanging near a horse's pounding hind legs. Maybe that's why Bonnie Williams became a trick rider and rodeo comedy-act specialist. After all, she grew up watching her mother ride broncs and bulldog steers.

So far it looks as if the rodeo committee has the easy

job. All they have to do is line up a good stock contractor, tell him what they need and then pay the bill when it comes due. If only it were that easy! Someone has to handle publicity and getting the grounds ready. Another thing, a lot of people are going to show up for the rodeo. They need help getting around and finding places to stay. That's the committee's job.

Rodeo time gives fans a chance to dress the part. In the background are the campers many visitors stay in.

How does a rodeo grow from a Lions Club or sheriff's posse member saying, "Say, what if we have a rodeo?" to the announcer calling out, "Ladies and gentlemen?" First, club members, chambers of commerce, private profit-making corporations, or nonprofit organizations must decide to give the undertaking a try. They do it because blind people, orphans, crippled children, medical research and other charities are often at the receiving end of the money the town realizes.

Many things determine whether a rodeo is going to be a success. Near the top of the list is the weather. Only a few cities have indoor arenas, and nothing dampens the spirit like a downpour or cold snap. If a town hasn't provided for visitors and contestants, word will get around. People are quick to cross a badly run rodeo off their list. They don't want to sit for hours waiting for the action to get rolling.

For the contestants one thing takes precedent over everything else. Are they treated fairly? Is the judging competent? Will there be enough prize money to make it worth the trip and entry fee? Contestants soon catch onto a rodeo that doesn't live up to its publicity. At the same time a rodeo that boasts the top contestants is the one that attracts the most fans. After all the best rodeos are made up of top athletes thrilling fans with great riding and roping ability.

ALL AROUND COWBOY CHAMPIONS 1929-1980

Earl Thode	1929	Casey Tibbs	1955
Clay Carr	1930	Jim Shoulders	1956
John Schneider	1931	Jim Shoulders	1957
Donald Nesbit	1932	Jim Shoulders	1958
Clay Carr	1933	Jim Shoulders	1959
Leonard Ward	1934	Harry Tompkins	1960
Everett Bowman	1935	Benny Reynolds	1961
John Bowman	1936	Tom Nesmith	1962
Everett Bowman	1937	Dean Oliver	1963
Burel Mulkey	1938	Dean Oliver	1964
Paul Carney	1939	Dean Oliver	1965
Fritz Truan	1940	Larry Mahan	1966
Homer Pettigrew	1941	Larry Mahan	1967
Gerald Roberts	1942	Larry Mahan	1968
Louis Brooks	1943	Larry Mahan	1969
Louis Brooks	1944	Larry Mahan	1970
No All-Around named	1945	Phil Lyne	1971
No All-Around named	1946	Phil Lyne	1972
Tod Whatley	1947	Larry Mahan	1973
Gerald Roberts	1948	Tom Ferguson	1974
Jim Shoulders	1949	Tom Ferguson	1975
Bill Linderman	1950	Tom Ferguson	1976
Casey Tibbs	1951	Tom Ferguson	1977
Harry Tompkins	1952	Tom Ferguson	1978
Bill Linderman	1953	Tom Ferguson	1979
Buck Rutherford	1954	Paul Tierney	1980

BAREBACK RIDING CHAMPIONS 1932-1980

(No Bareback Champions named by the R.A.A. until 1932.)

Smokey Snyder	*1932*	*Jim Shoulders*	*1956*
Nate Waldrum	*1933*	*Jim Shoulders*	*1957*
Leonard Ward	*1934*	*Jim Shoulders*	*1958*
Frank Schneider	*1935*	*Jack Buschbom*	*1959*
Smokey Snyder	*1936*	*Jack Buschbom*	*1960*
Paul Carney	*1937*	*Eddy Akridge*	*1961*
Pete Grubb	*1938*	*Ralph Buell*	*1962*
Paul Carney	*1939*	*John Hawkins*	*1963*
Carl Dossey	*1940*	*Jim Houston*	*1964*
George Mills	*1941*	*Jim Houston*	*1965*
Louis Brooks	*1942*	*Paul Mayo*	*1966*
Bill Linderman	*1943*	*Clyde Vamvoras*	*1967*
Louis Brooks	*1944*	*Clyde Vamvoras*	*1968*
Bud Linderman	*1945*	*Gary Tucker*	*1969*
Bud Spealman	*1946*	*Paul Mayo*	*1970*
Larry Finley	*1947*	*Joe Alexander*	*1971*
Sonny Tureman	*1948*	*Joe Alexander*	*1972*
Jack Buschbom	*1949*	*Joe Alexander*	*1973*
Jim Shoulders	*1950*	*Joe Alexander*	*1974*
Casey Tibbs	*1951*	*Joe Alexander*	*1975*
Harry Tompkins	*1952*	*Joe Alexander*	*1976*
Eddy Akridge	*1953*	*Joe Alexander*	*1977*
Eddy Akridge	*1954*	*Bruce Ford*	*1978*
Eddy Akridge	*1955*	*Bruce Ford*	*1979*
		Bruce Ford	*1980*

BULL RIDING CHAMPIONS 1929-1980

John Schneider	1929	Jim Shoulders	1955
John Schneider	1930	Jim Shoulders	1956
Smokey Snyder	1931	Jim Shoulders	1957
John Schneider	1932	Jim Shoulders	1958
Smokey Snyder	(tie)	Jim Shoulders	1959
Frank Schneider	1933	Harry Tompkins	1960
Frank Schneider	1934	Ronnie Rossen	1961
Smokey Snyder	1935	Freckles Brown	1962
Smokey Snyder	1936	Bill Kornell	1963
Smokey Snyder	1937	Bob Wegner	1964
Kid Fletcher	1938	Larry Mahan	1965
Dick Griffith	1939	Ronnie Rossen	1966
Dick Griffith	1940	Larry Mahan	1967
Dick Griffith	1941	George Paul	1968
Dick Griffith	1942	Doug Brown	1969
Ken Roberts	1943	Gary Leffew	1970
Ken Roberts	1944	Bill Nelson	1971
Ken Roberts	1945	John Quintana	1972
Pee Wee Morris	1946	Bobby Steiner	1973
Wag Blesing	1947	Don Gay	1974
Harry Tompkins	1948	Don Gay	1975
Harry Tompkins	1949	Don Gay	1976
Harry Tompkins	1950	Don Gay	1977
Jim Shoulders	1951	Don Gay	1978
Harry Tompkins	1952	Don Gay	1979
Todd Whatley	1953	Don Gay	1980
Jim Shoulders	1954		

CALF ROPING CHAMPIONS 1929-1980

Everett Bowman	1929	Dean Oliver	1955
Jake McClure	1930	Ray Wharton	1956
Herb Meyers	1931	Don McLaughlin	1957
Richard Merchant	1932	Dean Oliver	1958
Bill McFarlane	1933	Jim Bob Altizer	1959
Irby Mundy	1934	Dean Oliver	1960
Everett Bowman	1935	Dean Oliver	1961
Clyde Burk	1936	Dean Oliver	1962
Everett Bowman	1937	Dean Oliver	1963
Clyde Burk	1938	Dean Oliver	1964
Toots Mansfield	1939	Glen Franklin	1965
Toots Mansfield	1940	Junior Garrison	1966
Toots Mansfield	1941	Glen Franklin	1967
Clyde Burk	1942	Glen Franklin	1968
Toots Mansfield	1943	Dean Oliver	1969
Clyde Burk	1944	Junior Garrison	1970
Toots Mansfield	1945	Phil Lyne	1971
Royce Sewalt	1946	Phil Lyne	1972
Troy Fort	1947	Ernie Taylor	1973
Toots Mansfield	1948	Tom Ferguson	1974
Troy Fort	1949	Jeff Copenhaver	1975
Toots Mansfield	1950	Roy Cooper	1976
Don McLaughlin	1951	Roy Cooper	1977
Don McLaughlin	1952	Roy Cooper	1978
Don McLaughlin	1953	Paul Tierney	1979
Don McLaughlin	1954	Roy Cooper	1980

SADDLE BRONC RIDING CHAMPIONS 1929-1980

Earl Thode	1929	Deb Copenhaver	1955
Clay Carr	1930	Deb Copenhaver	1956
Earl Thode	1931	Alvin Nelson	1957
Pete Knight	1932	Marty Wood	1958
Pete Knight	1933	Casey Tibbs	1959
Leonard Ward	1934	Enoch Walker	1960
Pete Knight	1935	Winston Bruce	1961
Pete Knight	1936	Kenny McLean	1962
Burel Mulkey	1937	Guy Weeks	1963
Burel Mulkey	1938	Marty Wood	1964
Fritz Truan	1939	Shawn Davis	1965
Fritz Truan	1940	Marty Wood	1966
Doff Aber	1941	Shawn Davis	1967
Doff Aber	1942	Shawn Davis	1968
Louis Brooks	1943	Bill Smith	1969
Louis Brooks	1944	Dennis Reiners	1970
Bill Linderman	1945	Bill Smith	1971
Jerry Ambler	1946	Mel Hyland	1972
Carl Olson	1947	Bill Smith	1973
Gene Pruett	1948	John McBeth	1974
Casey Tibbs	1949	Monty Henson	1975
Bill Linderman	1950	Monty Henson	1976
Casey Tibbs	1951	Bobby Berger	1977
Casey Tibbs	1952	Joe Marvel	1978
Casey Tibbs	1953	Bobby Berger	1979
Casey Tibbs	1954	Clint Johnson	1980

STEER ROPING CHAMPIONS 1929-1980

Charles Maggini	1929	Clark McEntire	1957
Clay Carr	1930	Clark McEntire	1958
Andy Jauregui	1931	Everett Shaw	1959
George Weir	1932	Don McLaughlin	1960
John Bowman	1933	Clark McEntire	1961
John McIntire	1934	Everett Shaw	1962
Richard Merchant	1935	Don McLaughlin	1963
John Bowman	1936	Sonny Davis	1964
Everett Bowman	1937	Sonney Wright	1965
Hugh Bennett	1938	Sonny Davis	1966
Dick Truitt	1939	Jim Bob Altizer	1967
Clay Carr	1940	Sonny Davis	1968
Ike Rude	1941	Walter Arnold	1969
King Merritt	1942	Don McLaughlin	1970
Tom Rhodes	1943	Olin Young	1971
Tom Rhodes	1944	Allen Keller	1972
Everett Shaw	1945	Roy Thompson	1973
Everett Shaw	1946	Olin Young	1974
Ike Rude	1947	Roy Thompson	1975
Everett Shaw	1948	Charles Good, W	1976
Shoat Webster	1949	Marvin Cantrell, S	1976
Shoat Webster	1950	Guy Allen, W	1977
Everett Shaw	1951	Buddy Cockrell, S	1977
Buddy Neal	1952	Kenny Call, W	1978
Ike Rude	1953	Sonny Worrel, S	1978
Shoat Webster	1954	Gary Good	1979
Shoat Webster	1955	Guy Allen	1980
Jim Snively	1956		

STEER WRESTLING CHAMPIONS 1929-1980

Gene Ross	1929	Willard Combs	1957
Everett Bowman	1930	James Bynum	1958
Gene Ross	1931	Harry Charters	1959
Hugh Bennet	1932	Bob Robinson	1960
Everett Bowman	1933	Jim Bynum	1961
Shorty Ricker	1934	Tom Nesmith	1962
Everett Bowman	1935	Jim Bynum	1963
Jack Kerschner	1936	C.R. Boucher	1964
Gene Ross	1937	Harley May	1965
Everett Bowman	1938	Jack Roddy	1966
Harry Hart	1939	Roy Duvall	1967
Homer Pettigrew	1940	Jack Roddy	1968
Hub Whiteman	1941	Roy Duvall	1969
Homer Pettigrew	1942	John W. Jones	1970
Homer Pettigrew	1943	Billy Hale	1971
Homer Pettigrew	1944	Roy Duvall	1972
Homer Pettigrew	1945	Bob Marshall	1973
Dave Campbell	1946	Tommy Puryear	1974
Todd Whatley	1947	Frank Shepperson	1975
Homer Pettigrew	1948	Rick Bradley, W	1976
Bill McGuire	1949	Tom Ferguson, S	1976
Bill Linderman	1950	Tom Ferguson, W	1977
Dub Phillips	1951	Larry Ferguson, S	1977
Harley May	1952	Tom Ferguson, W	1978
Ross Dollarhide	1953	Byron Walker, S	1978
James Bynum	1954	Stan Williamson	1979
Benny Combs	1955	Butch Myers	1980
Harley May	1956		

TEAM ROPING CHAMPIONS 1929-1980

Charles Maggini	1929	Olan Sims	1951
Norman Cowan	1930	Asbury Schell	1952
Arthur Belcat	1931	Ben Johnson	1953
Ace Gardner	1932	Eddie Schell	1954
Roy Adams	1933	Vern Castro	1955
Andy Jauregui	1934	Dale Smith	1956
Lawrence Conley	1935	Dale Smith	1957
John Rhodes	1936	Ted Ashworth	1958
Asbury Schell	1937	Jim Rodriguez, Jr.	1959
John Rhodes	1938	Jim Rodriguez, Jr.	1960
Asbury Schell	1939	Al Hooper	1961
Pete Grubb	1940	Jim Rodriguez, Jr.	1962
Jim Hudson	1941	Les Hirdes	1963
Verne Castro	1942	Bill Hamilton	1964
Vic Castro	(tie)	Jim Rodriguez, Jr.	1965
Mark Hull	1943	Ken Luman	1966
Leonard Block	(tie)	Joe Glenn	1967
Murphy Chaney	1944	Art Arnold	1968
Ernest Gill	1945	Jerold Camarillo	1969
Chuck Sheppard	1946	John Miller	1970
Jim Brister	1947	John Miller	1971
Joe Glenn	1948	Leo Camarillo	1972
Ed Yanez	1949	Leo Camarillo	1973
Buck Sorrels	1950	H.P. Evetts	1974

Leo Camarillo	1975	George Richards, W	1978
Bucky Bradford, W	1976	Brad Smith, W	1978
Ronnie Rasco, W	1976	Doyle Gellerman, S	1978
Leo Camarillo, S	1976	Walt Woodard, S	1978
David Motes, W	1977	Allen Bach	1979
Dennis Motes, W	1977	Tee Woolman	1980
Jerold Camarillo, S	1977		

ARENA — the open area where the riding and timed events are held.

ASSOCIATION SADDLE — used for saddle bronc riding. Each saddle must have standard measurements. It is covered with soft sheepskin on the underside.

BAREBACK RIGGING — a double-thick leather pad for the contestant to sit on. Slightly off center at the top of the rigging is a leather handhold.

BULLDOGGER — another term for a steer wrestler. A contestant is said to "bulldog" a steer to the ground.

CHUTE — the area just outside the arena where broncs and bulls are kept before the event. The chute has high sides which allow the contestant to climb on the animal's back.

COWBELL — a large clanging bell which hangs between the bull's legs and is held in place by the manila rope which serves as the rider's handhold.

FAIR CATCH — any legal rope throw in a roping event.

FLANK STRAP — a sheepskin-covered strap placed around the bucking stock just in front of the hind legs and pulled tight just before the ride begins.

GOOSE EGG — no score for a ride.

GRA — Girls Rodeo Association, now the Womens Professional Rodeo Association.

HAZER — the contestant in steer wrestling who keeps the steer running straight ahead but doesn't try to wrestle it to the ground.

HEADER — the contestant in team roping who loops a rope around the animal's horns.

HEELER — the header's partner. This contestant's job is to rope both hind legs.

HEMP ROPE — the rein attached to a saddle bronc's halter. It is usually made of braided Manila some 6 feet long and an inch and a half thick.

LARIAT — the ropes used in roping events. They are made of twisted nylon.

PIGGING STRING — a slim six foot length of rope used to tie a calf's legs. Slightly longer and heavier ropes are used to tie steers.

PERMITTEE — a newcomer to the rodeo world who must prove him or herself by winning a set amount of money in a year's time in order to step up and become a professional.

POINTS — these are awarded in the riding events. The contestant is given points based on style of riding. The stock is also awarded points depending on how well it bucks. The total score is based on a combination of both.

PRCA — Professional Rodeo Cowboy Association, the men's organization.

RANK BULL — one which does everything possible to throw a rider. The rankest wind up as top bucking stock.

SCORE LINE — a barrier which the contestant in roping events has to remain behind until the calf or steer has been given a head start.

SUICIDE CIRCUIT — so called because keeping up with all the rodeos can sometimes be exhausting.

WPRA — Womens Professional Rodeo Association, the group most women contestants belong to.

Bruce Hunt and his quarterhorse are working as a team. The peggin string in Bruce's teeth will be used to tie the calf's legs.

ABOUT THE AUTHOR

Vella c Munn is a native Californian now living in Oregon, where she is the editor of the *Jacksonville Nugget,* a weekly newspaper. Besides editing and writing for the *Nugget* she has found time to write extensively for magazines.

She has been an avid rodeo fan for years and has covered the sport for newspapers and magazines. That interest led to this book, her first.

Besides her career as writer and editor she is a homemaker and the mother of two children. The family sporting interests include soccer, baseball and interscholastic wrestling.